May I Quote You, General Lee?

Other volumes in the
The May I Quote You, General . . . ? series

MAY I QUOTE YOU, GENERAL LEE?

Observations and Utterances of the South's Great Generals

VOLUME TWO

Edited by Randall Bedwell

CUMBERLAND HOUSE

NASHVILLE, TENNESSEE

May I Quote You...? is a Registered Trademark of Spiridon Press Press, Inc.

Some quotes have been edited for clarity and brevity.

Published by Cumberland House Publishing, Inc., 341 Harding Industrial Drive, Nashville, Tennessee 37211.

Managing Editor: Hollis Dodge

Senior Editor: Jimmy Vaden

Contributing Editors: Robert Kerr, Palmer Jones

Research Associate: Jim Fox

Typography: BookSetters

Text design: BookSetters

Cover design: Patterson Graham Design Group

Library of Congress Cataloging-In-Publication Data

May I quote you, General Lee? : observations and utterances from the South's greatest generals / edited by Randall Bedwell.

    p. cm. —(May I quote you, General? series)

    ISBN 1-888952-34-2 (pbk. : alk, paper)

    1. Lee, Robert (Robert Edward) 1807-1870—Quotations. 2. United States—History—Civil War, 1861-1865—Quotations, maxims, etc. 3. Quotations, American, I. Bedwell, Randall. J. II. Series.

E467.1.L47M46 1998

973.7'3'092—dc21   96-51927

                                           CIP

Printed in the United States of America

1 2 3 4 5 6 7 8—02 01 00 99 98

To my wife, Amanda Bedwell

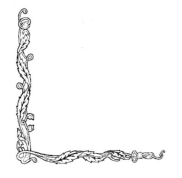
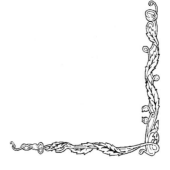

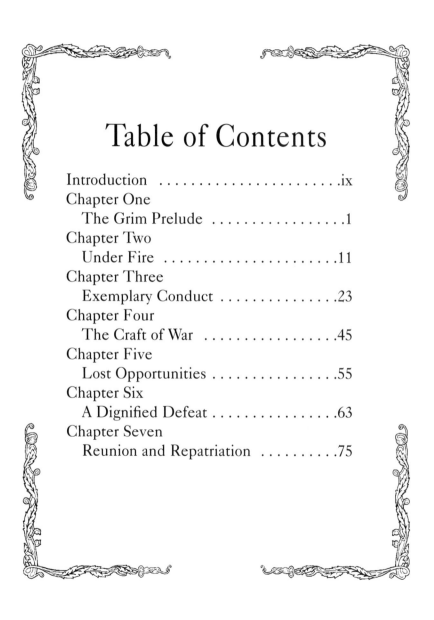

Table of Contents

Robert E. Lee was one
of the small company of great men
in whom there was no inconsistency to
be explained, no enigma to be solved. What
he seemed, he was—a wholly human gentleman,
the essential elements of whose positive
character were two and only two,
simplicity and spirituality.

—Douglas Southall Freeman,
Robert E. Lee's biographer

Introduction

The statements on these pages are among the most moving and insightful ever to express what Oliver Wendell Holmes Jr. called "the incommunicable experience of war." The South's great generals knew they were commissioned not only to win battles—though they did strive heroically and often triumphantly for victory. They were equally entrusted with a sacred responsibility to uphold duty and honor. Following the principled example set by General Robert E. Lee, the Southern command was characterized by gallantry and chivalry in the face of overwhelming odds. The Confederate generals represent a tradition that is now as far removed from contemporary experience as the way of life they fought to preserve. Their words are an immortal testament to their dignity.

Randall Bedwell
Nashville, Tennessee
October 1998

General Robert E. Lee

CHAPTER ONE

The Grim Prelude

In the days and weeks before discord boiled over into war, the generals and executives of the Confederacy refrained from inflammatory rhetoric. They could not indulge in the heady, reckless posturing adopted by so many private citizens during that period. The commanders knew what lay ahead. They knew their words would have consequence.

Instead of boasts and swagger, the South's sage leaders counseled temperance and reason. They viewed war as the sum of all evils. They warned of the North's determination and underlying strength, and the folly of firing on Fort Sumter.

Yet, their self-restraint never reflected any attempt to shirk their duty. In the end, service to their homeland decided their course.

Secession is nothing
but revolution. Still, a union
that can only be maintained by
swords and bayonets, and in which
strife and civil war are to take the
place of brotherly love and kindness,
has no charm for me. If the Union is
dissolved, the government disrupted,
I shall return to my native state and
share the miseries of my people.
Save in her defense, I will draw
my sword no more.

—Robert E. Lee, in a letter to his son, 1861

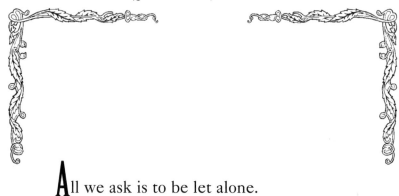

All we ask is to be let alone.

—*Jefferson Davis, president,*
Confederate States of America

It is painful enough to discover with what unconcern they speak of war and threaten it. I have seen enough of it to make me look upon it as the sum of all evils.

—*Stonewall Jackson, 1861*

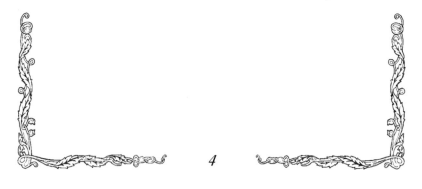

[If the] Northern states…desire to inflict injury upon us…a terrible responsibility will rest upon it, and the suffering of millions will bear testimony to the folly and wickedness of our aggressors.

—*Jefferson Davis, inaugural address as provisional president of the Southern Confederacy, February 18, 1861*

I am in favor of making a thorough trial for peace, and if we fail in this and our state is invaded, to defend it with terrific resistance.

—*Stonewall Jackson to his nephew, January 1861*

The North is determined to preserve this Union. They are not a fiery, impulsive people as you are, for they live in colder climates, but when they begin to move in a given direction, they move with the steady momentum and perseverance of an avalanche.

—*Texas Governor Sam Houston, 1861*

Unless you sprinkle blood in the face of the Southern people, they will be back in the old Union in less than ten days.

—*An advisor to Jefferson Davis*

The firing on that fort will inaugurate a civil war greater than any the world has ever seen. . . . It is unnecessary; it puts us in the wrong; it is fatal.

—*Confederate Secretary of State Robert Toombs*

I cannot raise my hand against my birthplace, my home, my children.

—*Robert E. Lee, in his letter of resignation from the U.S. Army*

I think it better to do right, even if we suffer in so doing, than to incur the reproach of our consciences and posterity.

—*Robert E. Lee*

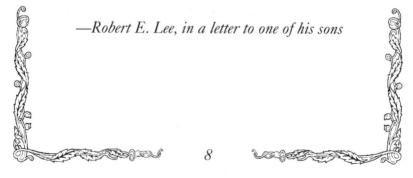

Our country demands all
our strength, all our energies.
To resist the powerful combination
now forming against us will require
every man at his place. If victorious,
we have everything to hope for in the
future. If defeated, nothing will be
left for us to live for. My whole
trust is in God, and I am ready
for whatever He may
ordain.

—*Robert E. Lee, in a letter to one of his sons*

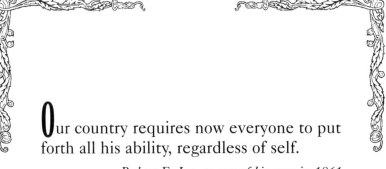

Our country requires now everyone to put forth all his ability, regardless of self.

—Robert E. Lee, to one of his sons in 1861

All I am and all I have is at the service of my country.

—Stonewall Jackson, 1861

I prefer annihilation to submission. They may destroy but I trust never conquer us.

—Robert E. Lee to a relative, 1861

James Longstreet

CHAPTER TWO

Under Fire

In the stress of battle, many prewar reputations were the first casualties. Braggadocio proved useless against the Union cannonade for many classroom and armchair generals. Nonetheless, the slow-to-anger Southern command typified by the fighting style of Robert E. Lee displayed an unshakable courage in combat that is admired and even emulated to this day.

When the battle call sounded, the generals answered. They led their charges to where the fire

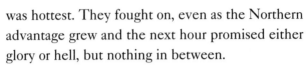

was hottest. They fought on, even as the Northern advantage grew and the next hour promised either glory or hell, but nothing in between.

These wartime leaders and the men they led dedicated themselves to preserving the South even if it cost them their lives.

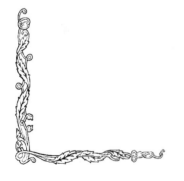
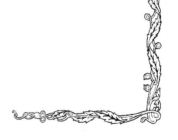

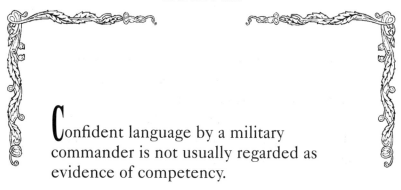

Confident language by a military commander is not usually regarded as evidence of competency.

—*Albert Sidney Johnston*

We will breakfast together here and dine together in hell.

—*Richard Stoddert Ewell at First Manassas*

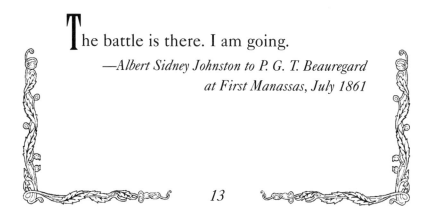

The battle is there. I am going.

—*Albert Sidney Johnston to P. G. T. Beauregard at First Manassas, July 1861*

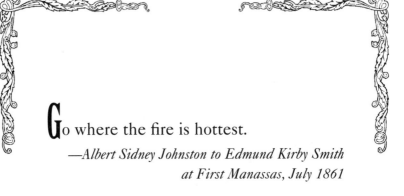

Go where the fire is hottest.

*—Albert Sidney Johnston to Edmund Kirby Smith
at First Manassas, July 1861*

Charge, men, and yell like furies!

*—Stonewall Jackson to his troops at
First Manassas, July 1861*

This is a hard fight and we had better all
die than lose it.

—General James Longstreet, Antietam, 1862

As each brigade
emerged from the woods,
from 50 to 100 guns opened
upon it, tearing great gaps in its
ranks; but the heroes pressed on
and were shot down by reserves
at the guns. It was not war; it
was murder.

—*D. H. Hill on the battle of Malvern Hill, 1862*

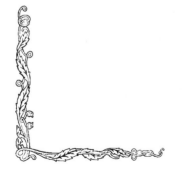

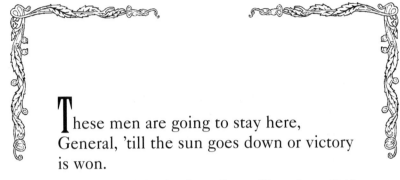

These men are going to stay here, General, 'till the sun goes down or victory is won.

—*John Gordon to Lee at Sharpsburg, 1862*

General, you have my hat and plume. I have your blue coat. I have the honor to propose a cartel for a fair exchange of the prisoners.

—*General J. E. B. Stuart to John Pope
after Stuart had lost his hat on a raid behind
Pope's lines but had stolen the Union
general's new coat in a supply dump.
Second Manassas 1862*

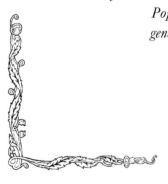

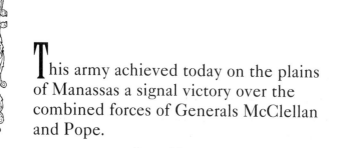

This army achieved today on the plains of Manassas a signal victory over the combined forces of Generals McClellan and Pope.

—General Lee to President Davis on the victory at Second Manassas, 1862

I think you hurt them as much as they hurt you.

—Longstreet to Lee on the Peninsula campaign and Seven Days' Battles in 1862

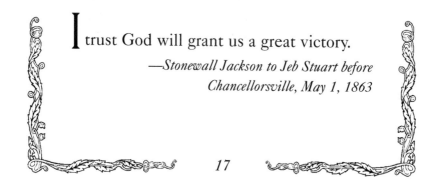

I trust God will grant us a great victory.

—Stonewall Jackson to Jeb Stuart before Chancellorsville, May 1, 1863

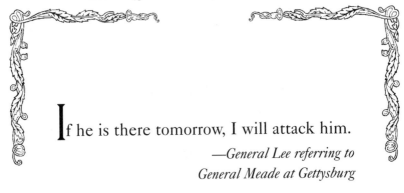

If he is there tomorrow, I will attack him.

—*General Lee referring to General Meade at Gettysburg*

In an hour, you'll be in hell or glory.

—*General Cadmus Marcellus Wilcox to General George Pickett at Gettysburg, 1863*

General Meade might as well have saved himself the trouble, for we'll have it in our possession before night.

—*General Lee on General Meade at Gettysburg*

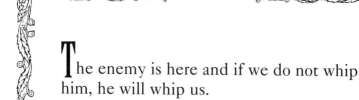

The enemy is here and if we do not whip him, he will whip us.

—*General Lee to General John Bell*
Hood at Gettysburg, 1863

General, if you are to advance at all, you must come at once or we will not be able to support you as we ought. . . . For God's sake, come quick.

—*E. P. Alexander to General Longstreet at*
Gettysburg just before Pickett's Charge

I consider it a privilege to die for my country.

—*Brigadier General Paul John Semmes, after*
being wounded at Gettysburg, July 1863

19

Our enemy is very cautious, and he has become so proficient in entrenching that he seems to march with a system already prepared. He threatens dreadful things every day, but, thank God, has not expunged us yet.

—General Lee on General Grant at Petersburg

Attention, Texas Brigade! The eyes of General Lee are upon you. Forward, march!

—General Maxcy Gregg at the Wilderness in 1864

Face the fire and go in where it is hottest!

—General A. P. Hill, May 1864

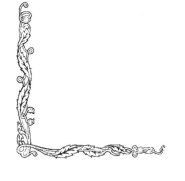

Nathan Bedford Forrest

CHAPTER THREE

Exemplary Conduct

In war as in peace, Robert E. Lee conducted himself in a manner that inspired devotion and emulation from his soldiers and fellow officers. His men considered him an agent of God, placed in their midst not only to lead them through battle but also toward a higher calling.

Although unassuming in manner and dress, Lee won the respect of both the soldiers under his command and those who fought against him. He was a man of patience, moderation and fortitude.

Throughout the struggle between the states, Lee counseled the South to maintain honor, duty and hope, even in its darkest hour.

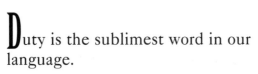

Duty is the sublimest word in our language.

—*Robert E. Lee*

The idea of his life was to do his duty, at whatever the cost, and to try to help others do theirs.

—*Robert E. Lee Jr., on his father*

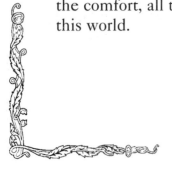

Do your duty. That is all the pleasure, all the comfort, all the glory we can enjoy in this world.

—*Robert E. Lee*

[Lee] came back, carrying the heavy weight of defeat, and unappreciated by the people, for they could not know that, if his plans had been carried out, the result would have been victory. Yet, through all this, he stood in silence, without defending himself for he was unwilling to offend any one who was wearing a sword and striking a blow for the Confederacy.

—Jefferson Davis on Lee in 1861 after Lee's campaign into the Shenandoah Valley

It will give me great pleasure to do everything I can to relieve him and serve the country, but I do not see either advantage or pleasure in my duties.

> —*General Lee writing in a letter to his wife about*
> *his replacing General Joseph Johnston, who*
> *had been wounded at Seven Pines, 1862*

What is life without honor? Degradation is worse than death.

> —*Stonewall Jackson to an officer who had*
> *requested a leave to visit a sick relative.*

I shall endeavor to do my duty and fight to the last.

> —*General Lee, in a letter to his wife, 1865*

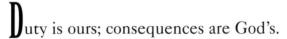

Duty is ours; consequences are God's.

—Stonewall Jackson

What do you care about rank? I would serve under a corporal if necessary!

*—General Lee's reproach to a
subordinate eager for promotion*

But what care can a man give to himself in time of war? It is from no desire of exposure or hazard that I live in a tent, but from necessity. I must be where I can speedily attend to the duties of my position, and be near or accessible to the officers with whom I have to act.

*—General Lee, in a letter to his wife,
September 18, 1864*

Eight million people turned their eyes to Lexington seeking instructions and paternal advice in the severe trials they have to undergo. They read in the example of General Lee . . . the lessons of patience, moderation, fortitude, and earnest devotion to the requirements of duty, which are the only safe guides to them in their troubles. His history, his present labors, and his calm confidence in the future kindle the flames of hope in the hearts of millions, that else all would be darkness.

—*John M. Morgan commenting on Robert E. Lee's unique position in the national consciousness after the war*

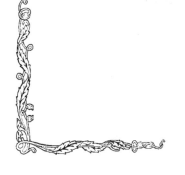

I am as willing to serve now as in the beginning in any capacity and at any post where I can do good. The lower the position, the more suitable to my ability and the more agreeable to my feelings.

—*General Lee to Jefferson Davis,*
after the Gettysburg defeat, 1863

My chief concern is to try to be an humble, sincere Christian.

—*Robert E. Lee*

Intellectually, he was cast in a giant mold. Naturally he was possessed of strong passions. He loved excitement, particularly the excitement of war. He loved grandeur. But all these appetites and powers were brought under the control of his judgment and made subservient to his Christian faith. This made him habitually unselfish and ever willing to sacrifice on the altar of duty and in the service of his fellows. . . . He is an epistle, written of God and designed by God to teach the people of this country that earthly success is not the criterion of merit, not the measure of true greatness.

—*General John Gordon on Robert E. Lee*

I can only say that I am nothing but a poor sinner, trusting in Christ alone for salvation, and need all of the prayers they can offer for me.

—General Lee's response when told that the army chaplains were daily praying for him.

I hope we will yet be able to damage our adversaries when they meet us. That it should be so, we must implore the forgiveness of God for our sins, and the continuance of his blessings.

—Robert E. Lee

The advantages of the enemy will have little value if we permit them to impair our resolution. Let us then oppose them with the firm assurance that He who gave freedom to our fathers will bless the efforts of their children.

—*Robert E. Lee, 1865*

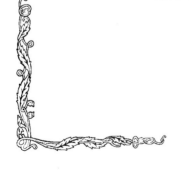

What a glorious world God Almighty has given us. How thankless and ungrateful we are, and how we labor to mar His gifts.

—Robert E. Lee

Mark the perfect man, and behold the upright; for the end of that man is peace."

—Psalm 37. William Nelson Pendleton (former Confederate chaplain) composed Lee's eulogy around this Bible passage

Through the broad extent of country over which you have marched by your respect for the rights and property of citizens, you have shown that you were soldiers not only to defend but able and willing both to defend and protect.

—*Stonewall Jackson to his troops, 1861*

I have never witnessed on any previous occasion such entire disregard of the usage of civilized warfare and the dictates of humanity.

—*General Lee, in a report concerning Union destruction of civilian property in Virginia, 1863*

All I ever wanted was a Virginia farm, no end of cream and fresh butter and fried chicken—not one fried chicken, or two, but unlimited fried chicken.

—*General Lee bantering with Mary Boykin Chesnut and friends just after First Manassas*

General Jubal Early to General Lee: I wish they were all dead.

Lee to Early: Why, I do not wish that they were all dead. I merely wish that they would return to their homes and leave us in peace.

Early, after Lee departed: I would not say so in front of General Lee, but I wish that they were not only dead but in hell.

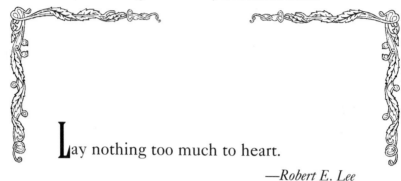

Lay nothing too much to heart.

—Robert E. Lee

Human virtue should be equal to
human calamity.

—Robert E. Lee

It is only the ignorant who suppose
themselves omniscient.

—Robert E. Lee

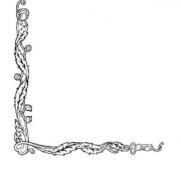

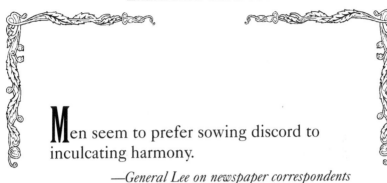

Men seem to prefer sowing discord to inculcating harmony.

—General Lee on newspaper correspondents

We have only one rule here—to act like a gentleman at all times.

—General Lee's only rule as president of Washington College

A true man of honor feels humble himself when he cannot help humbling others.

—Robert E. Lee

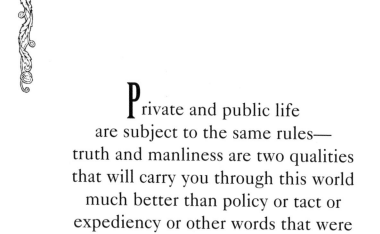

Private and public life
are subject to the same rules—
truth and manliness are two qualities
that will carry you through this world
much better than policy or tact or
expediency or other words that were
devised to conceal a deviation
from a straight line.

—*Robert E. Lee*

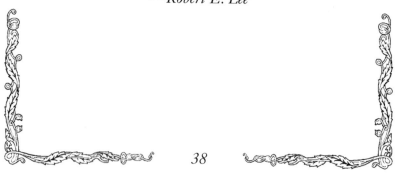

As a general principle, you should not force young men to do their duty, but let them do it voluntarily and thereby develop their characters.

—*Robert E. Lee*

The trite saying that honesty is the best policy has met with the just criticism that honesty is not policy. The real honest man is honest from conviction of what is right, not from policy.

—*Robert E. Lee*

Say what you mean to
do . . . and take it for granted
that you mean to do right. Never
do a wrong thing to make a friend or
keep one . . . you will wrong him and
wrong yourself by equivocation
of any kind.

—*Robert E. Lee*

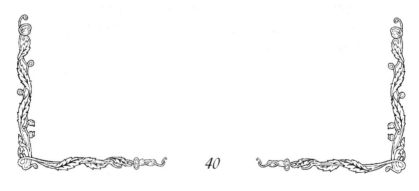

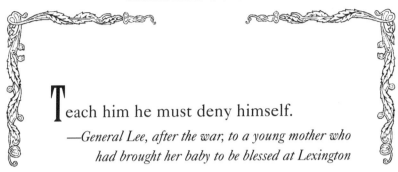

Teach him he must deny himself.

*—General Lee, after the war, to a young mother who
had brought her baby to be blessed at Lexington*

Practice self-denial and self-control, as
well as the strictest economy in all
financial matters.

—Robert E. Lee

He exhibited no external signs of his
rank, his dress being a plain suit of gray.
His office was simply furnished with plain
desks and chairs.

—A. L. Long on Lee

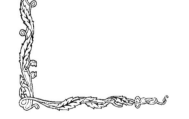

Read history, works
of truth, not novels and romances.
Get correct views of life, and learn to
see the world in its true light. It will
enable you to live pleasantly, to do
good and, when summoned away,
to leave without regret.

—*Robert E. Lee*

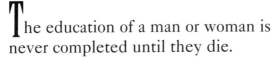

The education of a man or woman is never completed until they die.

—*Robert E. Lee*

He exhibited no external signs of his rank, his dress being a plain suit of gray. His office was simply furnished with plain desks and chairs.

—*A. L. Long on Lee in 1861*

You don't care for military glory or fame, but we are proud of your name and the record of this army. We want to leave it to our children. . . . A little blood, more or less, now makes no difference.

—*E. P. Alexander to Lee at Appomattox*

Joseph E. Johnston

CHAPTER FOUR

The Craft of War

Outnumbered and undersupplied, the South's generals employed innovative battle strategies that were often so brilliant they have been studied and utilized by military strategists for more than a century. Regardless of the circumstances, these Southern commanders resolutely directed their troops in a manner that would become legend.

Ultimately, however, the South's greatest generals are remembered most not for their military strategies but rather for their unwavering devotion to the basic tenets of duty.

His name might be Audacity. He will take more desperate chances and take them quicker than any other general in the country, North or South.

—General Ives on Lee

McClellan will make this a battle of posts. He will take position from position, under cover of his heavy artillery, and we cannot get at him without storming his works, which with our new troops is extremely hazardous.

—General Lee to Davis prior to the
Seven Days' Battles, June 1862

I am aware that the movement is attended with much risk, yet I do not consider success impossible, and shall endeavor to guard it from loss. . . . What occasions me most is the fear of getting out of ammunition.

—General Lee to President Davis on
the Maryland invasion, 1862

We can only act upon probabilities and endeavor to avoid greater evils.

—General Lee, in a letter to Stonewall Jackson

We must expect reverses, even defeats. They are sent to teach us wisdom and prudence, to call forth greater energies, and to prevent our falling into greater disasters.

—*Robert E. Lee*

So great is my confidence in General Lee that I am willing to follow him blindfolded.

—*Stonewall Jackson*

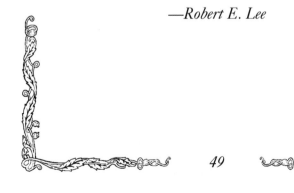

My interference in battle
would do more harm than good.
I have then to rely on my brigade and
division commanders. I think and work
with all my power to bring the troops
to the right place at the right time;
then I have done my duty. As soon as I
order them forward into battle. I leave
my duty in the hands of God.

—*Robert E. Lee*

If officers desire to have control over their commands, they must remain habitually with them, industriously attend to their instruction and comfort, and in battle lead them well.

—*Stonewall Jackson to his commanders, 1861*

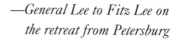

Keep your command together and in good spirits, General; don't let it think of surrender. I will get you out of this.

—*General Lee to Fitz Lee on the retreat from Petersburg*

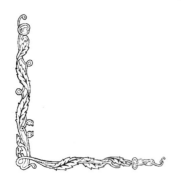

50

We may be annihilated, but we cannot be conquered.

—General Lee, in a letter to his brother, 1862

It is always well to expect the enemy to do what he should do.

—saying attributed to Lee

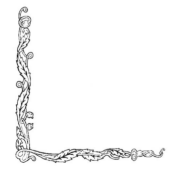

To move swiftly, strike vigorously, and secure all the fruits of victory is the secret of a successful war.

—Stonewall Jackson, 1863

I had rather lose one man in marching than five in fighting.

—Stonewall Jackson

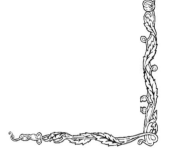

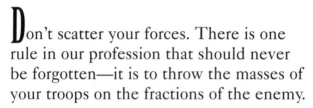

Don't scatter your forces. There is one rule in our profession that should never be forgotten—it is to throw the masses of your troops on the fractions of the enemy.

—William Joseph Hardee to
Braxton Bragg, October 7, 1862

Arms is a profession that, if its principles are adhered to for success, requires an officer do what he fears may be wrong and yet, according to military experience, must be done, if success is to be attained.

—Stonewall Jackson, in a letter to his wife, 1862

James Ewell Brown "Jeb" Stuart

CHAPTER FIVE

Lost Opportunities

Despite the storied exploits of Confederate troops that are retold and passed from generation to generation, there were also moments of hesitation and indecision that plagued the Southern command. In hindsight, the outcome of Gettysburg, and perhaps even the war, might have been different if other actions had been taken.

Unfortunately for them, generals are not granted the luxury of making their decisions in hindsight. Once written, history marches on, oblivious to all else that might have been.

Lee never tried to avoid blame; in fact, he insisted on shouldering more than he deserved. Most military historians have not judged him harshly; indeed, many consider him the greatest commander on either side of the war.

Our people have
thought too much of themselves
and their ease, and instead of turning
out to a man, have been content to
nurse themselves and their dimes
and leave the protection of
themselves and their families to
others. . . . This is not the way to
accomplish our independence.

—General Lee from South Carolina in 1861

I know Mr. Davis thinks that he can do a great many things that other men would hesitate to attempt. For instance, he tried to do what God had failed to do. He tried to make a soldier out of Braxton Bragg, and you know the result. It couldn't be done.

—*General Joseph Johnston*

When this war began I was opposed to it, bitterly opposed to it, and I told these people that unless every man should do his whole duty, they would repent it. And now they will repent.

—*General Lee speaking to his son*
Custis at Richmond in 1865

The Confederate chief at Gettysburg looked something like Napoleon at Waterloo.

—*James Longstreet on Lee*

If I had taken General Longstreet's advice on the eve of the second day of the battle of Gettysburg . . . [then] the Confederates would today be a free people.

—*Robert E. Lee*

Come General Pickett . . . this has been my fight and upon my shoulders rests the blame. The men and officers of your command have written the name of Virginia as high today as it has ever been written before.

—*General Lee at Gettysburg*

I never saw troops behave
more magnificently than Pickett's
division of Virginians did today in that
grand charge upon the enemy. And if
they had been supported as they were
to have been, the day would have
been ours.

—General Lee at Gettysburg

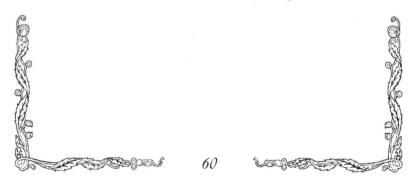

Over the splendid scene of human courage and human sacrifice at Gettysburg there arises in the South an apparition, like Banquo's ghost at Macbeth's banquet, which says the battle was lost to the Confederates because someone blundered.

—*Fitzhugh Lee*

If victorious, we have everything to live for. If defeated, there will be nothing left to live for.

—*General Lee, commenting on the outcome of the Wilderness campaign, 1863*

Stonewall Jackson

CHAPTER SIX

A Dignified Defeat

After four long years on the march and in battle, Lee faced the end in the spring of 1865. It was a conclusion the general had fought against with unsurpassed courage and fortitude despite overwhelming enemy numbers and superior resources. He declared he would rather "die a thousand deaths" than surrender.

With the eyes of the world watching, the Southern commanders and troops met the end with bitter tears, heads bowed, and heavy hearts.

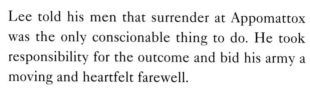

Lee told his men that surrender at Appomattox was the only conscionable thing to do. He took responsibility for the outcome and bid his army a moving and heartfelt farewell.

With that, Lee mounted his horse and rode away down a road lined with tearful Confederate soldiers.

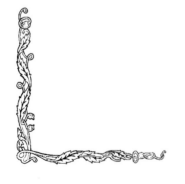

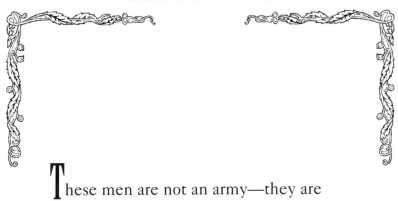

These men are not an army—they are citizens defending their country.

—*Robert E. Lee*

There is a true glory and a true honor; the glory of duty done—and the honor of the integrity of the principle.

—*Robert E. Lee*

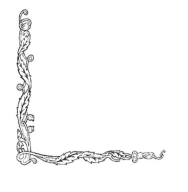

Yes, I know they will
say hard things of us; they will not
understand how we were overwhelmed
by numbers. But that is not the
question, Colonel; the question is,
"Is it right to surrender this army?" If
it is right, then I will take all
the responsibility.

—*General Lee at Appomattox*

There is nothing left me but to go and see General Grant, and I would rather die a thousand deaths.

—*General Lee on the morning of April 9, 1865*

As you are now more reasonable, I will say that General Lee has gone to meet General Grant, and it is for them to determine the future of our armies.

—*James Longstreet to General George A. Custer at Appomattox in response to the demand that Longstreet surrender the Army of Northern Virginia, April 9, 1865*

After four years of arduous service marked by unsurpassed courage and fortitude, the Army of Northern Virginia has been compelled to yield to overwhelming numbers and resources. With an unceasing admiration of your constancy and devotion to your country, and a grateful remembrance of your kind and generous consideration for myself, I bid you an affectionate farewell.

—*General Lee's farewell address to his army, April 10, 1865*

The road was packed by standing troops as he approached, the men with hats off, heads and hearts bowed down. As he passed, they raised their heads and looked upon him with swimming eyes. Those who could find voice said goodbye; those who could not speak, and were near, passed their hands gently over the sides of Traveller.

—James Longstreet at Appomattox

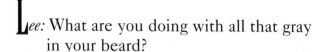

Lee: What are you doing with all that gray in your beard?

Meade: You have to answer for most of it.

—*April 10, 1865*

His continued self-denial can only be explained upon the hypothesis that he desired his men to know that he shared their privations to the very end.

—*Walter Taylor on General Lee en route
to Richmond after Appomattox*

It is utterly impossible, Mister Brady. How can I sit for a photograph with the eyes of the world upon me as they are today?

—*General Lee to Matthew Brady
at Richmond in 1865*

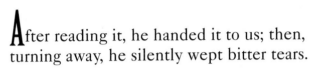

After reading it, he handed it to us; then, turning away, he silently wept bitter tears.

—Robert E. Lee III describing Jefferson Davis's reaction to the news of Lee's surrender to Grant

If I live, you can come to me when the struggle has ended, but I do not expect to survive the destruction of constitutional liberty.

—Jefferson Davis's parting words to his wife before the fall of Richmond

We had, I was satisfied, sacred principles to maintain and rights to defend, for which we were in duty bound to do our best, even if we perished in the endeavor.

—General Lee at the close of the war

I did only what my duty demanded. I could have taken no other course without dishonor. And if all were to be done over again, I should act in precisely the same manner.

—*Robert E. Lee*

It is fair to assume that the strongest laws are those established by the sword. The ideas that divided political parties before the war—upon the rights of states—were thoroughly discussed by our wisest statesmen, and eventually appealed to the arbitrament of the sword. The decision was in favor of the North, so that her construction becomes the law, and should be accepted.

—*James Longstreet*

We have fought this fight as long and as well as we know how. We have been defeated. For us, as Christian people, there is now but one course to pursue. We must accept the situation.

—General Lee after Appomattox

P. G. T. Beauregard

CHAPTER SEVEN

Reunion and Repatriation

After the war, Lee urged his countrymen to stop looking back. He counseled rejecting bitterness, accepting of the present and committing oneself to building a brighter tomorrow.

Bring up your children to be Americans, Lee told the fallen South. Now that the War Between the States had been fought and decided, maintaining allegiance to the Confederacy could serve no worthwhile purpose to anyone.

Lee may never have spoken words any wiser.

The thought of abandoning
the country and all that must be left in
it is abhorrent to my feelings, and I
prefer to struggle for its restoration and
share its fate rather than give up
all as lost.

—General Lee's response to suggestions that he leave
the country instead of live under Federal authority

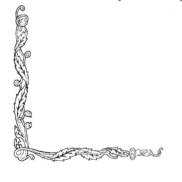

True Patriotism sometimes requires of men to act exactly contrary, at one period, to that which it does at another, and the motive which impels them—the desire to do right—is precisely the same.

—*Robert E. Lee*

I have fought against the people of the North because I believed they were seeking to wrest from the South its dearest rights. But I have never cherished toward them bitter or vindictive feelings, and have never seen the day when I did not pray for them.

—*Robert E. Lee*

I did believe at the time that [war] was an unnecessary condition of affairs and might have been avoided, if forbearance and wisdom had been practiced on both sides.

—*A portion of Lee's postwar testimony to the Congressional Committee on Reconstruction*

I can only judge by the past. I cannot pretend to foresee events.

—*excerpt of Lee's testimony before the Committee on Reconstruction, February 17, 1866*

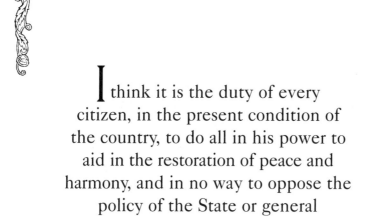

I think it is the duty of every citizen, in the present condition of the country, to do all in his power to aid in the restoration of peace and harmony, and in no way to oppose the policy of the State or general government directed to that object.

—General Lee's letter accepting the presidency of Washington College, August 24, 1865

I have led the young men of the South in battle; I have seen many of them die in the field; I shall devote my remaining energies to training young men to do their duty in life.

—*Robert E. Lee*

Madam, do not train up your children in hostility to the government of the United States. Remember, we are one country now. Dismiss from your mind all sectional feelings, and bring them up to be Americans.

—*General Lee as president of Washington College, Lexington, Virginia*

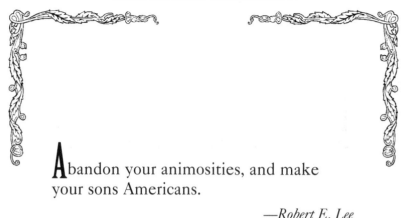

Abandon your animosities, and make your sons Americans.

—*Robert E. Lee*

Sir, if you ever again to presume to speak disrespectfully of General Grant in my presence, either you or I will sever his connection with this university.

—*General Lee speaking to a member of his board at Washington College, Lexington, Virginia*

Go home, all you boys who fought with me, and help to build up the shattered fortunes of our old state.

—General Lee, April 9, 1865

Go home and take up any work that offers. Accept conditions as you find them. Consider only the present and the future. Do not cherish bitterness.

—General Lee, speaking to soldiers and civilians alike in April 1865

Work is now
what we require, work by
everybody. . . . By this course the
good old times of former days . . . will
return again. We may not see them
but our children will, and we will
live over again in them.

—*Robert E. Lee*

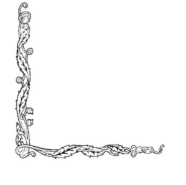

Christian faith
made him habitually
unselfish and ever willing
to sacrifice on the altar of
duty and the service
of his fellows.

*—General John Gordon speaking about
Lee after the war*

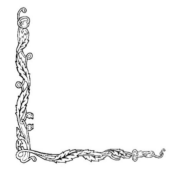

My own life has been written, but I have not looked into it. I do not wish to awaken memories of the past.

> —*General Lee, explaining that he never read a history of the Civil War or a biography of anyone who fought in it*

I'll never write my memoirs. I would be trading on the blood of my men.

> —*Robert E. Lee*

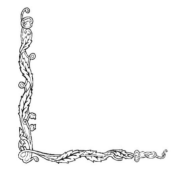